Irish Potato Cookbook

Irish Potato Cookbook

Eveleen Coyle

Gill & Macmillan

Gill & Macmillan Ltd
Hume Avenue, Park West
Dublin 12
with associated companies throughout the world
www.gillmacmillan.ie
© Eveleen Coyle, 1997, 2001
0 7171 3158 0
First published in this format 2001

Index compiled by Cover to Cover
Illustrations by Eva Byrne
Design by Slick Fish Design
Print origination by Carole Lynch
Printed by The Guernsey Press, Guernsey

This book is typeset in 9/14 pt Avenir.

*The paper used in this book is made from the wood pulp
of managed forests. For every tree felled, at least one tree is
planted, thereby renewing natural resources.*

A catalogue record for this book is available
from the British Library.

1 3 5 4 2

Contents

Introduction

Nothing can beat a pot of floury potatoes served with melting butter. But really they are at their best for only a few months of the year. In Ireland we love potatoes and eat them almost every day, all year round. Nutritious, rich in vitamin C, potassium and protein and low in cholesterol, potatoes should be a staple part of everyone's diet.

Assembling recipes for this book, it became clear how much our attitude to cooking generally and to potatoes in particular, has changed over the last decade. The combination of outside influences, traditional 'recipes-we-

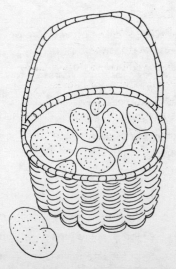

all-grew-up-with', and the necessity of putting a meal on the table for six people, six days a week: all these factors shaped the approach to cooking potatoes in my own household.

When the potato was introduced to Ireland in the early 17th century, it changed our whole way of life. Grown from seed potatoes laid in trenches or drills, the potato suited the stony and boggy land in a way that corn and grain crops, so popular in Europe, did not. Potatoes were less vulnerable to coastal winds and the yield was high. They grew in trenches, and trenches created good drainage on bogs. Drills could be dug in the most awkward bit of a field or on the seemingly inaccessible part of a mountain. A tiny plot could feed a family and help pay the rent, so small farmers quickly became dependent on potatoes.

By 1840, one-third of crops grown were potatoes. In 1845, potato blight hit Europe and spread swiftly to Ireland, destroying the crops for three years in a row. Over a million people died and many more emigrated. Walking anywhere in the West of Ireland today, the distinctive pattern of potato trenches abandoned since the Famine of 1845 is still clearly visible.

The range of potatoes available on the Irish market is vast and increasing all the time. The most common of the main-crop varieties are Home Guard (first early), Golden Wonders (my own favourite of the late main crop potatoes), Records,

Kerr's Pink, Pentland Dell, King Edward's, Arran and more recently, Roosters. In Ireland generally, we tend to prefer good floury potatoes rather than the waxy varieties favoured in other European countries.

This book both reflects our traditional cooking and acknowledges those recipes from friends, family, magazines and favourite cookery writers. Wherever I remember a source it is mentioned; some recipes have changed so much with use that they barely resemble the original.

Enjoy them all!

Buying and storing

- It is essential to choose carefully the best quality potatoes and to store them well.
- It is best to buy potatoes in small quantities that you will use quickly.
- Look for firm potatoes with no damp patches or wrinkly bits.
- Keep them in a dark, cool, airy place.
- If they are bought in plastic bags, remove the potatoes from the bag once you get home.
- Potatoes bruise easily so treat them gently.

Cooking tips

- As a general rule, allow about 225 g/8 oz of potatoes per person, but use your common sense and bear in

mind the people you are feeding, how you are cooking
the potatoes, and what you are serving them with, and
adjust your quantities accordingly.

- The same applies to cooking times and temperatures;
  take into account the size of the potatoes and the
  vagaries of your own oven.

- Try steaming potatoes rather than boiling them, particularly new potatoes.

- If you do boil them, pour on boiling water, return to
  the boil straight away and watch them carefully.

- Use as little water as possible because it steals nutrients
  from the potatoes.

- With older potatoes, start in lightly salted cold water
  and bring to the boil.

- A little fresh mint or a squeeze of lemon juice prevents
  after-cooking discolouring.

- Do not prepare potatoes in advance; above all, do not peel and leave them sitting in water for any length of time. If you must get them ready in advance, dry them and put them in a plastic bag in the bottom of the fridge to reduce discolouration.
- Eat potatoes unpeeled as far as possible — they are much more nutritious and a lot less trouble.
- If you do peel potatoes, use a sharp potato peeler. Remember the best part is just under the skin so you don't want to lose it.
- When I refer to salt and pepper, I mean good quality sea-salt and freshly ground pepper, black unless specified.
- Always season to your own taste. And taste all the time.

Common varieties available in Ireland

Potatoes tend to fall into three categories:

First Earlies Available June – July
Second Earlies Available July – August
Main Crop Available September – May

- Home Guard — a first early crop, white-fleshed potato. They are good for boiling, roasting, and new potato salads.
- Queens — second early, delicious floury potatoes, good for all uses.

- Golden Wonder — dry, floury, russet-skinned potatoes, one of the best of the late main crop potatoes.
- Kerr's Pink — another late main crop potato with a lovely pink skin. Also dry and floury.
- Records — main crop potato, dry and floury with yellow flesh.
- Pentland Dell — a main crop potato with creamy white flesh, a bit soapy but good for baking, chips etc.
- King Edward — another main crop potato with creamy flesh, good for roasting, chipping and boiling.
- Rooster — a main crop potato that is good for most methods of cooking.

1
Soups

Soup can be the best of meals or the most ordinary, depending on your ingredients. A well-made soup is nourishing, inexpensive and satisfying. Soups can be served as a snack, starter or made into a simple meal.

They can also be made in advance, using a variety of ingredients and enhanced with just about any herbs. It is worth keeping white and brown stock and fish stock (frozen in ice-cubes for convenience) in the freezer. Good quality stock cubes are available now, but beware, they

are often very salty. A blender is useful for mixing ingredients and getting the right texture, but it is not essential.

Simple, well-made potato soup is quick to prepare and has a lovely flavour. It can also form the base for many other soups.

POTATO SOUP
SERVES 4

This is a traditional soup recipe. It is both useful and tasty and can be served with various garnishes on top: cheese, parsley, chives or streaky rashers, fried crispy and crumbled. A good stock improves the flavour.

- 1 large onion, chopped
- 2 tbsp butter or bacon fat
- 200 g/10 oz potatoes, peeled and chopped
- 900 ml/1½ pints/3¾ cups chicken or beef stock
- 125 ml/4 fl oz/½ cup milk or cream
- salt and pepper
- chopped parsley to serve

Sweat the onion in butter, add the potatoes and cook for 10 minutes. Turn them gently and frequently but do not allow them to brown. Add the stock and simmer until the potato is tender. Purée in the blender and add milk or cream. Reheat, check the seasoning, stir in the parsley and serve.

POTATO AND LEEK SOUP
SERVES 6

- 450 g/1 lb leeks
- 3 tbsp butter
- 450 g/1 lb potatoes, peeled and chopped
- 1.2 litres/2 pints/5 cups chicken stock
- salt and pepper

Chop the leeks into 2.5 cm/1 inch pieces, soak them in cold water to clean, then drain. Melt the butter in a heavy-based saucepan and add the leeks. Cover with grease-proof paper and a tight lid. Sweat until the leeks are soft. Add the potato, cover and cook for a further 10 minutes, watching carefully so they do not burn. Add the stock and simmer for 30 minutes until the potato is cooked. Season well, liquidise and serve piping hot with fresh crusty bread.

POTATO AND SORREL SOUP
SERVES 4

This is an unusual soup with a terrific sharp flavour. I got the recipe originally from Lindsey Bareham's wonderful book *In Praise of the Potato*.

- 4 tbsp butter
- 400 g/14 oz sorrel leaves, washed and stalks removed
- 1 small onion, chopped
- 1 shallot, chopped
- 450 g/1 lb potatoes, peeled and diced
- 900 ml/1½ pints/3¾ cups chicken stock
- salt and pepper

Melt the butter in a heavy-based saucepan and add the sorrel. Cover and sweat until the leaves wilt and turn dark green. Add the onion and shallot, cook for a couple of minutes, add the potatoes and stock. Simmer for 40 minutes until the potatoes are done. Liquidise, season and garnish with croûtons and cream to serve.

POTATO AND ONION SOUP
SERVES 4

This is a really handy recipe simply because most of us always have potatoes and onions in the house.

- 2 tbsp butter
- 450 g/1 lb onions, peeled and chopped
- 225 g/½ lb potatoes, peeled and diced
- 1 tbsp chopped parsley
- 900 ml/1½ pints/3¾ cups chicken stock
- 150 ml/¼ pint/⅔ cup milk or top-of-the-bottle milk
- salt and pepper

Melt the butter in a heavy saucepan, add the onions and potatoes and coat well with butter. Add the parsley and seasoning. Cover tightly with greaseproof paper under the lid and let them sweat for about 10 minutes until they are tender but not brown. Add the stock, bring to the boil, add milk and boil gently until the potatoes are cooked. Season to taste with salt and pepper.

POTATO SOUP WITH BACON AND VEGETABLES

SERVES 4–6

This soup should be thick, chunky and rich. The smoked bacon on top gives it a lovely flavour.

- 75 g/3 oz/6 tbsp butter
- 900 g/2 lb potatoes, peeled and diced
- ¼ head celeriac, diced
- 2 medium carrots, diced
- 900 ml/1½ pints/3¾ cups chicken or vegetable stock, or water
- 1 leek cut lengthways and sliced
- 1 onion, diced
- 300 ml/½ pint/1¼ cups cream or cream and milk mixed, optional
- pinch of freshly ground nutmeg
- salt and pepper
- 75 g/3 oz smoked bacon
- croûtons
- 1 scallion (US green onion) cut into thin strips

Heat 55 g/2 oz/4 tbsp of butter in a heavy saucepan and sauté the potatoes, celeriac and carrots. Cover with cold water or stock, bring to the boil and simmer for about 40 minutes. Purée half the soup by putting it through a sieve or liquidiser. Heat the remainder of the butter in a pan, sauté the leek and onion lightly (be careful not to overcook or burn them), and combine with the purée and the rest of the soup. Add the cream (I don't like milk or cream in soup, so I just add extra stock or water), season with the nutmeg, salt and pepper and cook for a further 5 minutes. Dice the bacon and brown it in the butter-coated pan. Serve the soup with the croûtons, diced bacon and scallion sprinkled on top.

The following two recipes make wonderful, old-fashioned cold-weather soups, filling and warming.

WINTER SOUP
SERVES 6–8

- 900 ml/1½ pints/3¾ cups water
- 900 ml/1½ pints/3¾ cups stock
- 170 g/6 oz/¾ cup brown lentils
- 170 g/6 oz/¾ cup peeled and finely diced potato
- 2 carrots, diced
- 75 g/3 oz/¾ cup diced onions
- 3 celery sticks, diced
- 45 g/1½ oz/⅓ cup fine oatmeal
- 250 ml/8 fl oz/1 cup milk
- salt, pepper and nutmeg to taste

Put the water and stock into a saucepan and add the lentils and potato. Bring to the boil, add the remaining vegetables, then the oatmeal blended with a little water. Stir gently until boiling again, then occasionally until it is cooked — about 45 minutes. Add the milk and seasoning. Liquidise the soup. Boil it up again before serving piping hot.

POTATO AND VEGETABLE SOUP
SERVES 6

- blade of mace
- bouquet garni (parsley, sage and thyme tied in a bunch)
- 2 tbsp bacon fat or butter
- 1 large potato, peeled and chopped
- 1 onion, chopped
- 1 carrot, chopped
- 3 sticks celery, chopped
- 1.8 litres/3 pints/7½ cups light stock
- 55 g/2 oz/¼ cup brown lentils, rinsed
- 30 g/1 oz ground rice
- salt and pepper
- 250 ml/8 fl oz/1 cup half-milk, half-cream

Add a blade of mace to the bouquet garni. Melt the fat in a saucepan, add the vegetables, and toss. Cook gently until they have absorbed the fat but not browned. Add the stock and bouquet garni. Add the lentils and simmer for 45 minutes. Remove the bouquet garni and liquidise. Return to the saucepan and thicken with the ground rice. Season, boil again, add the milk and cream and serve.

MINESTRONE SOUP WITH PESTO
SERVES 8

This soup is not quick to make but is worth every bit of effort. It appeals to me because it calls for fresh borage, which I always seem to have far too much of and never use, except to put the lovely blue flowers in a salad.

- 225 g/8 oz dried white haricot beans
- 3.6 litres/6 pints/7½ US pints water
- 1 large onion, roughly chopped
- 2 sticks celery, sliced
- 1 carrot, sliced
- 6 tbsp olive oil
- 2 medium courgettes, sliced
- 4 medium tomatoes, peeled and roughly chopped
- 4 large potatoes, peeled and chopped
- 3 leaves fresh borage, finely chopped
- 225 g/8 oz macaroni, elbow shaped
- 2 tbsp pesto sauce
- 6 tbsp grated Pecorino or other sharp cheese

Soak the haricot beans overnight and partially cook in unsalted boiling water. Drain the beans and put in a big saucepan with the water. Add the onion, celery, carrot and 4 tbsp of oil and simmer for about an hour. Add the courgettes, tomatoes, potatoes and borage. Bring back to the boil and cook for a further half-hour. Add the macaroni and cook for about 15 minutes or until the macaroni is just done. Then stir in the pesto with the remainder of the oil, add the cheese and serve at once in warm dishes with good crusty bread.

VICHYSSOISE

SERVES 4

Not traditional to Ireland, perhaps, but very good and easy to make. Once more, try to use good stock. It makes a difference to the delicate flavour and creamy consistency of this soup. A stock cube won't do!

- 170 g/6 oz potatoes, peeled and sliced
- 3 large leeks, white part only, sliced
- 1 stick celery, sliced
- 2 tbsp butter
- 1.2 litres/2 pints/5 cups good chicken or vegetable stock
- salt and pepper
- 150 ml/¼ pint/⅔ cup cream
- 1 tbsp chopped chives

Sweat all the vegetables in the butter until just soft. It is a good idea to put a little greaseproof paper under the lid of the saucepan when sweating vegetables. They must be soft but not coloured, so keep your eye on them and stir occasionally. Stir in the stock, bring to the boil and simmer for about 15 minutes. Liquidise or rub through a sieve. The soup must be smooth. Season and stir in the cream. Leave the soup to get cold, then whisk for a few minutes and chill. Serve sprinkled with chives.

PROVENÇAL POTATO SOUP
SERVES 4

This has become a favourite with everyone in our house. I first came across it in Robert Carrier's *Gourmet Vegetarian* book. New potatoes are especially good.

- 1 tbsp olive oil
- 2 tbsp finely chopped onions
- 1 clove of garlic, finely chopped
- 450 g/1 lb potatoes, thickly sliced
- 2 pinches of saffron
- 900 ml/1½ pints/3¾ cups vegetable stock or water
- 3–4 basil leaves, torn
- 3 Italian tomatoes, peeled
- salt and pepper
- 4–6 strips of sundried tomatoes (in oil)

Heat the oil in a saucepan, add the onion and garlic and sauté until they are transparent but not brown. Add the potatoes and cook over a medium heat, coating the potatoes with the oil. Add the saffron and leave for about a minute, then the stock, basil leaves, tomatoes, salt and pepper. Simmer for about 20 minutes. Finally add a few strips of the sundried tomato and cook until the potatoes are tender.

POTATO, TOMATO AND LEEK SOUP
SERVES 4–6

- 2 tbsp butter
- 225 g/½ lb young leeks
- 450–900 g/1–2 lb good tomatoes, peeled and chopped
- 450 g/1 lb potatoes, peeled and diced
- salt and pepper
- 750 ml/1¼ pints/3 cups light stock or water
- 60 ml/2 fl oz/¼ cup cream or top-of-the-bottle milk
- fresh chervil or basil to serve

Melt the butter in a heavy pan and cook the leeks gently until soft, then add the tomatoes and cook until the juice starts running. Toss in the potatoes, season and cover with the stock. Bring to the boil and simmer for about 20 minutes until the potatoes are cooked. Purée, check the seasoning, return to the pan and bring back to the boil slowly. Add the cream and serve at once, garnished with chervil or chopped basil.

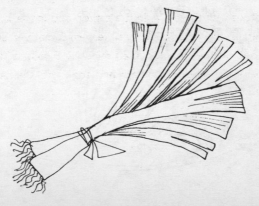

Stock

Stock is simple to make, costs just about nothing and is one of the most useful items to have in your freezer. I freeze it in the ice-cube tray and then put the cubes into bags; that way you can use as little or as much at a time without having to get out the ice-pick.

CHICKEN STOCK

- chicken bones/carcass/giblets
- 1½ cups vegetables such as carrot/leeks/celery
- 1 medium onion
- 6 peppercorns
- bay leaf — optional
- salt

If you are using the carcass, break it up, then chop the vegetables. Place all ingredients in a saucepan, add enough water to cover, bring to the boil, skim if necessary and then simmer for about 1½–2 hours. Strain, allow to cool and skim the fat off. It is now ready to use. I don't use a bay leaf in chicken stock because I find the flavour too strong, but suit your own taste. This makes about 2 pints.

BEEF OR BROWN STOCK

- 450 g/1 lb shin beef cut into pieces
- 450 g/1 lb marrow bones
- bouquet garni
- 1 onion, peeled and sliced
- 1 carrot, chopped
- 1 stick celery
- salt

Brown the meat and bones in the oven before adding them to the stock to improve the colour, about 30 minutes in a roasting pan in a hot oven (220°C/425°F/Gas 7). Put all ingredients in a saucepan and cover with water. Bring to the boil, skim and simmer for about 4 hours. Strain, allow to cool and then remove any fat from the top before using or freezing.

FISH STOCK

- 450–675 g/1–1½ lbs fish bones and trimmings
- salt
- bouquet garni
- onion

Put the fish bones in a saucepan, cover with 600 ml/1.2 litres/1–2 pints of water and bring to the boil. Before adding the other ingredients, skim off the top. Simmer for about 30 minutes and then cool. Fish stock does not keep very long even in the fridge so if you are not using it the same day it is best to freeze it.

VEGETABLE STOCK

Most vegetable trimmings can go into vegetable stock so the following is just a guideline.

- 1 onion
- 1 carrot
- 1 turnip
- 3 celery sticks
- vegetable trimmings
- bouquet garni
- salt
- 6 black peppercorns

Peel and chop the root vegetables and chop the celery sticks. Heat a little oil in a saucepan and gently fry the onion until soft. Add all the other vegetables, cover with water and bring to the boil. Simmer for about 2 hours. Strain and leave to cool.

2

Old Favourites

The problem with mashed, boiled, baked, steamed or roast potatoes is that all too often little thought goes into their preparation. Although simple, they are often difficult to get just right. Firing potatoes into a hot oven around a lump of meat does not guarantee good roast potatoes — and lumpy mashed potatoes should be outlawed.

The following recipes are basic and offer variations which you can try depending on your own taste. In all recipes it is worth choosing a variety of potato suitable for the dish you are preparing, as some potatoes hold together better than others.

Mashed potatoes

Choose floury old potatoes for mashing, for example Kerr's Pinks, Golden Wonders or King Edwards. Select potatoes of approximately the same size. Put them in a saucepan of lightly salted cold water, bring to the boil and boil carefully, uncovered or partly covered, until they are cooked. If you can bear to peel hot potatoes, boil them in their skins — it does improve the flavour. If you can't, peel them first and boil them even more carefully as they tend to break up easily.

TRADITIONAL MASHED POTATOES
SERVES 6

- 900 g/2 lb potatoes
- 2 tbsp butter
- 90 ml/3 fl oz/⅓ cup top-of-the-bottle milk or half-milk and half-cream or milk
- salt and pepper

Scrub the potatoes, bring them to the boil and cook until just done. While they are cooking, warm the milk and cream. Drain the potatoes, peel quickly and shake them over the heat to dry out. Mash them with a hand masher, adding the butter and the warmed milk and cream. Season to taste.

MASHED POTATOES 2
SERVES 6

The flavour of these is quite different to potatoes mashed with butter. The olive oil is all important. If you use oil the quality of car oil, the potatoes will taste of car oil, so use a good quality fruity oil for this recipe. It is very good with grilled or barbecued meat.

- 900 g/2 lb potatoes
- 2 tbsp good fruity olive oil
- 90 ml/3 fl oz/⅓ cup cream or top-of-the-bottle milk
- salt and pepper

Scrub the potatoes well, bring to the boil and cook until tender. Drain and peel the potatoes, add the olive oil, cream and salt and pepper. Mash well together and taste for seasoning. Serve piping hot.

MASHED POTATOES
WITH FRESH HERBS
SERVES 6

Make sure that your herbs are fresh and dry. If herbs are damp when you are chopping them they will bruise easily, and won't look so good when added to the hot mashed potato.

- 900 g/2 lb potatoes
- 2 tbsp butter
- 90 ml/3 fl oz/⅓ cup top-of-the-bottle milk or half-milk and half-cream or milk
- salt and pepper
- 8 tbsp chopped parsley
- 8 tbsp chopped chives

Scrub the potatoes well and boil in salted water until tender. Drain, peel and mash the potatoes, add the butter, cream and seasoning and mash again. Beat in the parsley and chives with a wooden spoon. Taste for seasoning. Serve in a hot bowl with a little melting butter in the centre.

Variations

Scallions, spinach (finely chopped) or good streaky rashers fried to a crisp all make a wonderful addition to mashed potatoes and can be used instead of the herbs suggested above. Choose carefully and don't mix too many flavours. Also bear in mind what you plan to serve with them.

MASHED POTATOES WITH ONIONS
SERVES 4

This is a nice recipe, but it is essential to cook the onion until it is soft: a mouthful of uncooked onion is not pleasant in this dish.

- 2 lb/900 g potatoes
- 1 large fresh onion, finely chopped
- 1 tbsp sunflower oil
- 4 tbsp butter
- salt and pepper
- 1 tbsp chopped parsley

Scrub the potatoes and cook in salted boiling water until tender. Meantime soften the onion in oil but do not allow it to brown. When the potatoes are cooked, peel and mash them well with butter, salt and pepper. Add the softened onion and parsley and mix well. Serve immediately in a hot dish.

MASHED POTATOES WITH PARMESAN AND OLIVE OIL

SERVES 4

Darina Allen is one of Ireland's best cooks and her *Simply Delicious* series has changed the way we look at food. This is one her recipes from *Simply Delicious Versatile Vegetables*. Parsley Salad is a very good accompaniment.

- 900 g/2 lb old potatoes
- 225 ml/8 fl oz/1 cup milk
- 4 tbsp extra virgin olive oil
- 55 g/2 oz/½ cup fresh Parmesan cheese, grated
- salt and pepper

Cook the potatoes in salted boiling water until almost done. Pour off most of the water, cover and steam for the rest of the cooking time. Boil the milk and add the olive oil to it. Mash the potatoes, add half the hot milk and oil, the Parmesan and then the rest of the milk. Season. Make sure the potatoes are well mashed and light.

Parsley Salad

- 110 g/4 oz/2 cups flat-leafed (or curly) parsley
- 75 g/3 oz/¾ cup Parmesan cheese shavings

French dressing made with

- 3 tbsp olive oil
- 2 tsp white wine vinegar
- 1 clove of garlic mashed with salt
- salt and pepper

Wash the parsley and dry it well. Combine the olive oil, vinegar, garlic, salt and pepper in the bottom of a salad bowl and mix well. Add the parsley and Parmesan, mix again and serve.

Roast Potatoes

What kind of roast potatoes do you like? If you like waxy potatoes, firm throughout, then choose Pentland Dell with its pale creamy flesh, or the more yellow and endlessly versatile Rooster. Kerr's Pinks, Golden Wonders and Records are floury and they crisp up beautifully.

A roasting pan with a heavy base is a good investment. Potatoes for roasting should be put in a pan of oil so hot that it is almost spitting at you, but don't allow it to burn. Remember that roast potatoes absorb the flavour of the oils, herbs or meat they are cooked with. If the oil is not really hot, the potatoes will be greasy. Coat them with hot fat and turn them at least once during roasting to ensure even cooking and colour. They should be cooked in a hot oven (220°C/425°F/Gas 7) and will take 45 minutes to

1 hour depending both on their size and your oven. Roast potatoes don't keep well, so serve them at once.

ROAST POTATOES 1
SERVES 6

Every family has the *only* recipe for really good roast potatoes and in our house, these are Matthew's favourite. We roast them the following way.

- 1.4 kg/3 lb good floury potatoes, peeled
- hot fat
- salt and pepper

Boil up freshly salted water, add the potatoes, bring back to the boil and simmer with the lid off for 5 minutes. Drain and dry them off in the saucepan by holding them over the heat. Replace the saucepan lid and shake vigorously to roughen up the outside. Heat the oil in a roasting pan and add the potatoes; baste them all over and sprinkle with salt and pepper. Roast for about 45 minutes in a hot oven (220°C/425°F/Gas 7), turning at least once. The outside will then be beautifully crisp. If you use particularly floury potatoes for this recipe they will disintegrate slightly and won't look like the perfect roast potato — but they taste luscious!

ROAST POTATOES 2
SERVES 6

This is a more sober roast potato. The outside is less crisp and the inside firm and well behaved. It tends not to fall apart in the roasting pan so looks good, but we think it's much duller. The lesser quantity of potato used than in the previous recipe seems to feed the same number of people, which says it all. The same rules apply.

- 900 g/2 lb peeled potatoes
- hot oil or fat, for roasting
- salt and pepper

Peel the potatoes and put them straight into the hot oil or fat, either around the meat or in a roasting pan on their own. Cook in a hot oven (220°C/425°F/Gas 7) for at least 45 minutes, basting and turning the potatoes a couple of times during cooking. Test with a skewer and sprinkle with sea-salt and pepper just before they are cooked. Serve in a hot bowl or on a large meat dish arranged around the roast.

ROAST POTATOES WITH GARLIC AND BUTTER
SERVES 6

This is simple and very good if you like garlic. It loses its sharpness cooked this way with the potatoes — even the most garlic-resistant people can be caught eating it.

- 900 g/2 lb potatoes, well scrubbed
- 2 tbsp olive oil
- 2 tbsp butter
- salt and pepper
- head of garlic

Scrub the potatoes very well, making certain
to get rid of the eyes. In the meantime
heat the butter and oil in a roasting pan
in the oven. Add the potatoes with a
little salt and pepper.
Roast in a hot oven
(220°C/425°F/Gas 7)
for about 25 minutes,
basting and turning
once. Add the garlic
broken up into cloves
but unpeeled. Roast for a further 15 minutes, by which time
the potatoes will be cooked through and brown. The garlic should be deliciously creamy and come away from the
skin easily.

ROAST POTATOES WITH
GARLIC AND ROSEMARY
SERVES 6

This recipe comes from Italy and is delicious with spring
lamb or chicken. The rosemary is very good in it and not
too strong.

- 900 g/2 lb medium-sized unpeeled potatoes, scrubbed
  and quartered
- 4 tbsp hot oil
- 3 sprigs of rosemary
- salt and pepper
- head of garlic

Scrub the potatoes well and quarter them. They don't need to be peeled unless the skin is very coarse. Toss them in hot oil in a roasting pan, strip the rosemary sprigs and sprinkle the spikes over the potatoes with the salt and a little pepper. Break up the head of garlic and add cloves to the roasting pan. Cook in a very hot oven (220°C/450°F/Gas 7) for about 30 minutes, turning once. These potatoes are full of flavour; they smell irresistible and look terrific too.

ROAST POTATOES WITH BAY LEAVES
SERVES 8

Home Guard from the first early potatoes are great for this recipe, although any small and evenly-sized potato will do. My husband adores these and cooks them regularly. They are particularly good with game, and handy for entertaining. You can parboil and prepare them with the bay leaf in advance, then put them in the oven when it suits you.

- 1.4 kg/3 lb small even-sized potatoes
- 10–12 bay leaves
- 4 large cloves of garlic, unpeeled
- 6 tbsp olive oil
- salt and pepper

Scrub the potatoes well but don't peel them. Cook in boiling water for 3–4 minutes, then drain and cool slightly. Carefully cut a slit in half of the potatoes and insert a bay leaf in each. Meanwhile place the garlic and olive oil in a large roasting pan and put in a hot oven (220°C/ 425°F/Gas 7) for a few minutes to heat the oil well. Add the potatoes and make sure they are well coated in the olive oil. Season with coarse salt and coarsely ground pepper. Roast for 35–40 minutes or until cooked.

ROAST POTATOES WITH BREADCRUMBS AND PARMESAN
SERVES 6

My children love these although I find them a bit fiddly to make. Be careful not to overcook them or the breadcrumbs and cheese taste like burnt toast.

- 900 g/2 lb potatoes
- 1 egg, lightly beaten
- 55 g/2 oz/½ cup freshly grated Parmesan cheese
- 55 g/2 oz/1 cup dry breadcrumbs
- salt and pepper
- 2–3 tbsp extra virgin olive oil

Peel and parboil the potatoes for about 10 minutes. Drain and shake them dry in the saucepan. Brush or dip them in egg, then in the Parmesan mixed with seasoned bread-crumbs. Meantime heat the oil in a roasting pan in a hot oven (220°C/425°F/Gas 7). Add the potatoes and quickly baste to seal them. Cook until they are tender and golden, about 40 minutes depending on size.

ROAST NEW POTATOES WITH BACON, GARLIC, THYME AND ROSEMARY
SERVES 4

These are simple to do and full of flavour. If you are using new potatoes, try to get Home Guards: they are the best for this recipe by a long shot. Timing depends on the size of your potatoes and you can, of course, use older potatoes.

- 450–800 g/1–1¾ lb small new potatoes
- 4–6 cloves of garlic
- 110 g/4 oz good streaky bacon, chopped
- 4 sprigs of thyme
- 4 sprigs of rosemary
- 3 tbsp olive oil

Scrub the potatoes well. If you choose main crop potatoes, use same-size ones, and because they will take longer to cook, don't add the herbs until half-way through the cooking or they will burn. Place the potatoes, garlic and herbs in a roasting pan and toss in oil. Roast in a preheated oven (220°C/425°F/Gas 7) for 20–30 minutes. Drain and sprinkle with coarse salt.

Steamed Potatoes

New potatoes are lovely but tend mostly to be soapy and are always better steamed. In Ireland we get a lot of 'new' potatoes imported from Italy and Cyprus, but our own Home Guards are the best for flavour and consistency.

Just scrub them well, sprinkle with a little salt and place on a well-fitting steamer with a good lid to steam until they are tender. Remove from the heat, take off the lid and place a clean tea-cloth on top to absorb some of the steam and to make them a little less soapy.

NEW POTATOES WITH MINT AND CHIVES
SERVES 4

New potatoes with butter, mint and chives can make you feel that summer has arrived, even if the weather is a bit doubtful. The smell of chopped tender mint leaves and young chives fills the kitchen, and the flavour is hard to beat. If you have never invested in a good quality, decent-sized steamer, do it now.

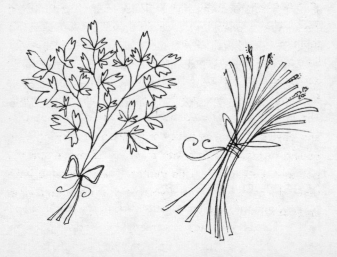

- 900 g/2 lb new potatoes
- 2 tbsp butter
- 2 generous tbsp chopped fresh mint
- 2 generous tbsp chopped fresh chives
- salt and pepper

Scrub the potatoes well, place in a steamer with a good-fitting lid and steam for 15–20 minutes or until tender. Dry off and place in a hot bowl. Melt the butter, remove from the heat, add the herbs and season. Pour over the potatoes and serve at once. These are also good cold.

Baked Potatoes

Choose good floury potatoes such as King Edwards or Golden Wonders. Scrub them thoroughly and dry them well. Prick them with a skewer, and rub all over with a little melted butter or olive oil and rock salt. Place them on a roasting pan in a hot oven (220°C/425°F/Gas 7) and bake for about 1 hour — large ones can take up to 1¼ hours. The baking time will depend on the size of the potatoes and anyway baking is a slower method of cooking than boiling or roasting. Test with a skewer to make sure the potatoes are cooked in the middle. The slower you bake them, the crisper the skin. If you prefer a softer skin, wrap and bake them in tin foil.

BAKED POTATOES WITH SOUR CREAM, PARSLEY AND CHIVES
SERVES 6

Allow 1 large potato per person, or 2 for the more hungry members of your household. They are a great lunch-time snack on a cold day, or for children just in from school who can't wait for dinner.

- 6 large potatoes
- 1 small clove of garlic
- 2–3 tbsp sour cream or butter
- 1 tbsp chopped parsley
- 1 tbsp chopped chives
- salt and pepper

Scrub the potatoes, prick the top with a skewer and place on a baking sheet in a hot oven (220°C/425°F/Gas 7) for 1 hour or until cooked. While they are cooking, skin the garlic and mash it with a little salt until it is smooth. Blend it into the sour cream, add the herbs and season. Serve as a topping with baked potatoes.

BAKED POTATOES WITH CHEESE AND BACON
SERVES 6

- 6 large potatoes
- 110 g/4 oz good white Cheddar cheese, grated
- 2 slices of streaky bacon, fried and chopped
- 1 tbsp cream

- 1 tbsp butter
- salt and pepper

Scrub the potatoes well and bake them in a hot oven (220°C/425°F/Gas 7) for 45–60 minutes. When the potatoes are tender, halve them and carefully remove the flesh, making sure to keep the skins intact. Mash the flesh and place in a saucepan with the cheese, bacon, cream and butter. Heat and season carefully — you may not need salt, depending on the bacon. Put the mixture back into the skins, grill for 1 minute and serve.

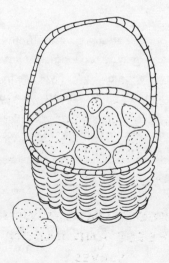

Chips

It seems to me that every child in the whole world adores chips, and adults follow close behind, but they all like different chips. In our house one member of the family swoons over McDonald's; another loves fat greasy chips from a bad chipper; yet another likes chips as chips should be — crisp on the outside and soft, melt-in-the-mouth inside. Except for Conor. Conor just likes chips — any chips please and delight him.

Floury potatoes are best for chips. Prepare them a little in advance by peeling the potatoes and cutting them into 5 cm/2 inch-thick strips. Leave them sitting in cold salty water to get rid of some of the starch and to give a crisper chip. If you haven't time to do that, rinse them very well under a cold tap.

Frying needs your full attention. Aside from burning food that is left in even a minute too long, an unattended pan of sizzling fat is very dangerous. When you are frying, don't be mean with the oil: use plenty of it and make sure it is clean. Don't mix your oils. When you have finished frying, allow the oil to cool, then strain it into a clean glass jar so that it is ready for the next time.

Put the oil in the pan and heat slowly until it is very hot but not smoking. Test the temperature with a chip — it should sizzle the minute it hits the oil and stay at the top of the saucepan. It is important not to overcrowd the pan: add only as many as the pan can comfortably take. Chips will take about 7–10 minutes to cook, and you should shake the pan gently now and then during the cooking. Lift them out of the pan and dry them off on warmed kitchen paper or newspaper.

TRADITIONAL CHIPS
SERVES 4

- 900 g/2 lb floury potatoes
- oil
- salt and pepper

Peel the potatoes and cut lengthways, roughly 1.2 cm/ ½ inch wide. Soak them in a bowl of salted water for about 10 minutes. Drain and dry thoroughly on a clean tea towel. Heat the oil until very hot (180°C/350°F) but be careful not to allow it to smoke. Add the chips and cook for about 7 minutes until they are beginning to brown but not crisp. Shake the pan gently, allow to cook for another couple of minutes and then lift the chips out of the oil. Dry off on warm kitchen paper and serve quickly, lightly sprinkled with salt. Some people prefer freshly ground black pepper to salt.

If you wish, cook the chips in the hot oil for 5 minutes, lift them, dry them on kitchen paper and keep them aside for a while. When required, heat the oil again and fry the chips for about 5 minutes, or until they are hot and crisp. Then drain in the usual way.

Like roast potatoes, chips do not keep well. Serve them immediately.

BEST CHIPS IN THE WORLD
SERVES 4

In our house, Alice cooks these chips all the time and maintains this is the only way to cook them!

- 900 g/2 lb floury potatoes, unpeeled
- oil
- herbes de Provence
- salt

Scrub the potatoes thoroughly and cook in boiling water for about 10 minutes. Drain and cut into large chips. Heat the oil until it is very hot. While the oil is heating, rinse the chips in cold water and dry thoroughly. Fry the chips until they are brown and crispy, about 5 minutes. Remove them from the fat and dry them in heated newspaper. Sprinkle with herbes de Provence and salt. Serve immediately.

SAUTÉED POTATOES
SERVES 4

Sautéed potatoes is a great way of using up left-over potatoes. They need attention in the cooking, and should be fried slowly over a gentle heat rather than at a high temperature.

- 675 g/1½ lb cooked potatoes
- 2 tbsp butter
- salt and pepper

Slice the cooked potatoes, leaving the skin on if you wish. Heat the butter in a heavy pan, add the potatoes and cook slowly over a low heat until they are done, about 15–20 minutes. Turn them at least once during cooking. The potatoes should be a pale golden colour and crumbly on all sides. Drain them on warmed kitchen paper or newspaper. Season lightly and serve.

For a bit of variation you can add some finely chopped herbs such as parsley, tarragon (lovely if you are serving them with chicken) or rosemary.

SAUTÉED GARLIC POTATOES
SERVES 6

Each time my friend Monica McInerney writes to me from Australia, she encloses a recipe. The following one for sautéed new potatoes came from her; it is different and lovely.

- 900 g/2 lb new baby potatoes
- 2 cloves of garlic
- salt
- 4 tbsp butter
- 2 tbsp grated lemon rind
- 2 tbsp chopped parsley

Scrub and steam the potatoes until they are tender; drain and dry off. This can be done in advance and kept covered in the fridge until you need them. Skin the cloves of garlic and crush with a little salt until smooth. Heat the butter in a heavy-based frying pan, add the garlic and potatoes and cook gently until the potatoes are golden brown. Put them in a large warm bowl, add the lemon rind and parsley and toss them carefully. Serve immediately.

3
Main Courses

Many of the recipes in the chapter entitled 'Side Dishes' could validly be included in this section and vice versa. Most of the recipes here include meat or fish, with a couple of exceptions.

IRISH STEW
SERVES 6

There are endless variations on and disagreements about the correct ingredients for Irish Stew — for example, does real Irish Stew include carrots? And what about thyme? It grows wild all over the country, so in the past it probably was included. This recipe is the one I had as a child and still have at home. It probably originated from a book my mother used called the *Tailteann Cookery Book*. I add carrots if I have them and vary the quantities as it suits me.

- 900 g/2 lb neck end or gigot chops of lamb, cut into thick pieces
- 3 onions, sliced
- salt and pepper
- 4–6 good-sized potatoes, peeled and quartered
- 600 ml/1 pint/2½ cups brown stock or water
- chopped parsley

Put a layer of lamb on the bottom of a heavy casserole dish. I do not remove the bones before cooking simply because they add flavour and separate so easily from the meat when they are cooked. Follow with a layer of onions, salt and pepper and a layer of potatoes. Repeat this until all the ingredients are used up, finishing with potatoes. Add the stock or water and bring to the boil. Simmer gently for about 1½ hours or place in a slow oven for the same time. It is best not to let it cook too quickly: watch it carefully if you are cooking on top of the stove.

Irish Stew is greasy so if you have time, drain off the liquid, allow it to cool and skim off the fat. Put the liquid back and bring to the boil. If you haven't removed the bones, you can easily do so now, just using a fork. Or you can serve it and let people do it for themselves. Replace the liquid and heat it again. Sprinkle with parsley and serve.

FISH CAKES
SERVES 4

These are handy, economical and always tasty, especially for children who are reluctant to try 'ordinary' fish. You can use most fish for this basic recipe and although I have given quantities here, you will find this is one of those handy dishes that suits whatever you have in stock. I frequently vary the quantity of fish to potato, and use whatever herbs are to hand — chives, parsley or fennel. A clove of garlic well crushed is also good in fish cakes.

- 340 g/12 oz potatoes
- 225 g/8 oz cooked fish such as cod or salmon
- 55 g/2 oz butter
- 1 egg, beaten
- salt and pepper
- 2 tbsp chives, finely chopped
- 55 g/2 oz/1 cup dry breadcrumbs

Cook and mash the potatoes. Remove the bones or skin from the fish and add to the mashed potato. Add melted butter and a *little* beaten egg to bind the mixture. It needs only a little egg, otherwise it will be runny and difficult to cook. Season with salt and pepper and mix in the chives. Divide the mixture into little flat cakes. Dip in the egg and cover with breadcrumbs. Heat the oil in a pan and cook the fish cakes quickly for a couple of minutes on each side. They should be golden and crisp on both sides.

DUBLIN CODDLE
SERVES 4–6

Coddle is not my most favourite meal, but it is tasty and simple to make. Although considered a traditional dish, it is not made very much now; however it is beginning to appear on menus of some of the trendier restaurants around town. This is a good recipe which comes from Theodora FitzGibbon's *Irish Traditional Food*.

- 1 litre/1¾ pints/4½ cups water
- 8 thick slices of ham or bacon
- 8 large pork sausages
- 4 large onions, peeled and sliced
- 900 g/2 lb potatoes, peeled and sliced
- salt and pepper
- 4 tbsp chopped parsley

Bring the water to the boil and drop in the ham or bacon and sausages, cut into large chunks. Cook for 5 minutes, drain and reserve the water. Place the ham and sausages in a large saucepan or casserole dish, add the onions, potatoes, salt, pepper and half the parsley. Add enough of the reserved liquid to just cover. Place greased paper on top, cover with a lid and then either simmer gently or cook in a slow oven for about 1½ hours, until the liquid has reduced and everything is cooked. Serve in hot bowls.

Theodora suggests serving coddle with soda bread and a glass of Guinness.

SHEPHERD'S PIE
SERVES 4

This is usually made with beef left over from the Sunday joint, or any other meat. It tastes quite different when raw beef is used, indeed many would argue that, made from raw beef, it is not Shepherd's Pie at all but Cottage Pie.

- 2 tbsp butter
- 1 medium onion, chopped
- 2 carrots, sliced
- 4 tbsp flour
- 600 ml/1 pint/2½ cups good brown stock
- chopped parsley and thyme
- 450 g/1 lb cooked minced beef or lamb
- 675 g/1½ lb mashed potatoes

Melt the butter in a saucepan and add the chopped onion. Cover and let it sweat for a few minutes. Add the carrots. Stir in the flour and cook until it is slightly browned. Then add the stock and herbs, bring to the boil and reduce it a little by boiling for about 5 minutes. Add the meat and bring it back to the boil. Place in a pie dish and cover with the mashed potatoes. Put into a medium hot oven (180°C/350°F/Gas 4) for about 30 minutes.

Good Cheddar cheese grated on top 10 minutes before the end of the cooking time is lovely on this dish.

VEGETABLE CHEESE PIE
SERVES 6

This dish is lovely and the base is the most useful one you will find. The recipe was given to me by Kate Strathern. I don't know where she got it, but it is versatile and tasty. I vary the filling depending on which vegetables are in season. Getting the base crisp is the key to this dish.

- 340 g/12 oz/2 cups grated raw potato
- 1 tsp salt
- 1 large onion, grated
- beaten egg

Put the grated potato in a colander, add salt and leave for 10 minutes. Squeeze the excess liquid off and add the potato to the other ingredients. Pack the mixture into a deep well-buttered 23 cm/9 inch pie dish, building up the sides. Bake in a fairly hot oven (200°C/400°F/Gas 6) for 40–45 minutes until browned. After the first 30 minutes brush the pie with oil to crisp it up.

Filling

- 110 g/4 oz/1 cup chopped onion
- 1 medium clove of garlic, crushed
- 3 tbsp butter
- 2 tsp chopped fresh basil
- a little chopped fresh thyme
- 1 medium cauliflower, broken into florets
- 110 g/4 oz/1 cup grated Cheddar cheese
- ½ tsp salt
- 2 eggs and 50 ml/2 fl oz/¼ cup milk beaten together
- black pepper and paprika

Sauté the onions and garlic in butter for 5 minutes. Add the herbs and cauliflower and cook, covered, for 10 minutes, stirring occasionally. Season. Spread half the cheese on to the baked crust, followed by the sauté and the remaining cheese. Pour the beaten milk and egg over it and dust with paprika. Bake for 35–40 minutes in a slightly lower oven (190°C/375°F/Gas 5).

FISH PIE
SERVES 6

This is a good, rich pie using cod, but you could use any other white fish. It is given as a basic pie recipe in George Lassalle's terrific book *The Adventurous Fish Cook*. You will find that that is exactly how it works — the more you use it, the more you will adapt it to your own tastes. Using fish stock rather than water does make a difference in this dish — and it is easy to prepare.

- 675 g/1½ lb cod
- 2 hard-boiled eggs, finely chopped
- 1 heaped tbsp chopped parsley and capers, mixed
- 2 tbsp butter

- 4 tbsp flour
- 1 litre/1⅔ pints/4 cups fish stock or water
- 1 glass white wine
- salt and pepper
- 450 g/1 lb potatoes, boiled and mashed

Poach the fish for about 5 minutes, then remove from the water. If you have no fish stock, keep this water, add some carrot, celery, onion and bouquet garni, and leave to simmer while you are preparing the rest of the dish.

Remove any small bones from the fish, break it up gently and place in a big dish. Add the eggs and sprinkle with the herbs and capers. Melt the butter, stir in the flour carefully and add the warmed stock and wine. Bring to the boil and cook for about 20 minutes, allowing the stock to reduce by about half. Season and pour over the fish.

Add butter to the mashed potatoes and spread over the fish. Cook in a medium oven (180°C/350°F/Gas 4) for 25 minutes. The potatoes should be golden brown.

CHICKEN CASSEROLE WITH LEEKS AND GARLIC
SERVES 4

This is quicker to cook than it sounds and is good and filling. It is one of those recipes that appear in every cookery book you pick up; some recipes suggest adding a glass of wine, some use onions or other vegetables instead of leeks.

- 1 tbsp butter
- 675 g/1½ lb leeks, washed and sliced
- 1 tbsp flour
- 200 g/7 oz cream cheese with herbs and garlic
- 300 ml/½ pint/1¼ cups chicken stock
- 8 chicken thighs
- salt and pepper
- 450 g/1 lb potatoes, washed and sliced thinly

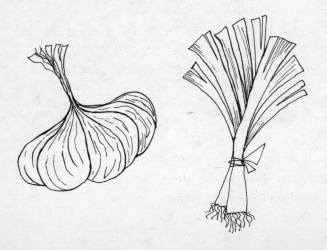

Heat the butter in a heavy-based dish and cook the leeks gently until they are soft but not brown. Meantime blend the flour into the cheese and add the stock (you could do this in the blender). Remove the leeks from the heat and arrange the chicken thighs on top. Pour the stock and cheese mixture over it and season well.

Layer the potatoes on top and cover them lightly with buttered foil (just cover, don't seal). Cook in a moderate oven (180°C/350°F/Gas 4) for 1–1½ hours. Remove the tin foil from the top of the potatoes for the last 20 minutes to give a nice golden finish.

BAKED NEW POTATOES WITH ANCHOVY AND PARSLEY

SERVES 4

This recipe comes from Sophie Grigson's *Eat Your Greens*. It is a really good lunch dish served with crusty bread and, yes, a salad of green leaves.

- 900 g/2 lb small new potatoes
- 3 tbsp olive oil
- 3 tbsp butter
- 2 or 3 anchovies
- 2 cloves of garlic, crushed with a little salt
- 2 tbsp chopped fresh parsley
- 150 ml/5 fl oz/⅔ cup water
- 2 tbsp lemon juice
- salt and pepper

Scrub the potatoes and pat dry. Heat the oil and butter in a heavy-based roasting pan. Add the anchovy fillets and cook for 1 minute, mashing the anchovy fillets into the oil with a fork. Add the potatoes and fry for a few minutes until they are beginning to colour. Add the garlic, parsley and water, followed by the lemon juice, salt and pepper. Bake in a fairly hot oven (200°C/400°F/Gas 6) for about 20 minutes, basting once. Serve in a hot dish and pour over the juice from the pan.

POTATOES WITH ASPARAGUS, BEANS AND PARMESAN
SERVES 4

This recipe came from a magazine a long time ago. It is very rich and makes a filling main course dish but it's important to use good cheese.

- 225 g/½ lb new potatoes
- good bunch of asparagus
- 225 g/½ lb broad beans — fresh or frozen
- 6 medium eggs
- salt and pepper
- 55–75 g/2–3 oz/½–¾ cup freshly grated Parmesan cheese
- 3 tbsp chopped herbs, e.g. parsley, thyme, tarragon or another*
- 4 tbsp butter

*Rosemary is nice, or tarragon, but tarragon is strong so don't use it unless you like it.

Scrub and steam the potatoes until just done. Leave to cool before cutting into thick slices. Trim the asparagus and steam for 12 minutes before dipping into cold water quickly. Prepare the broad beans. Drain the asparagus and cut into short lengths.

Put the eggs in a bowl with salt, pepper and half the Parmesan cheese. Beat until well blended and then stir in the beans, asparagus and herbs. Melt half the butter in a heavy-based pan. When it foams, add the egg mixture and turn down the heat. Allow to cook very slowly for 10–15 minutes or until set at the bottom but with the top a bit runny.

Put the sliced potatoes over the top, sprinkle the remaining Parmesan on them and dot the remaining butter over it. Place under a very hot grill until the top begins to brown. Do not take your eye off it at this point or it will become dry and leathery. Cut into thick wedges and serve at once.

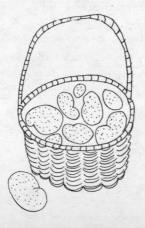

POTATO CASSEROLE
SERVES 4

It is important to blanch the green pepper for this recipe otherwise it is too strong, so if you are going to take a shortcut, choose some other one.

- 675 g/1½ lb small new potatoes
- 2 tbsp olive oil
- 225 g/½ lb onions
- 1 clove of garlic, finely chopped
- 2 tsp paprika pepper
- 2 tsp flour
- 2 tbsp wine vinegar
- 150–300 ml/¼–½ pint/⅔–1¼ cups good white stock
- salt and pepper
- 1 green pepper, blanched and chopped
- 2 tomatoes, skinned and deseeded
- 2 tbsp yoghurt or soured cream

Cook the potatoes in boiling water for 15 minutes. Heat the oil in a heavy casserole dish, add the onions and garlic, cook until golden but not brown. Stir in the paprika and cook for a further minute. Remove from the heat and blend in the flour, vinegar and enough stock to thicken. Season and bring to the boil. Drain the potatoes and add to the casserole with the green pepper and tomatoes. Cook for a further 5–10 minutes until the potatoes are done. Before serving, spoon in the yoghurt and stir gently.

SAUSAGE AND POTATO PIE
SERVES 4

This is a real winter dish which my husband, Fergus, who generally avoids 'pies', cooks and loves. It is very tasty and quick to make.

- 900 g/2 lb floury potatoes
- 450 g/1 lb pork sausages (Italian are best)
- 6 tbsp butter
- 2 tbsp chopped parsley
- 300 ml/½ pint/1¼ cup milk, warmed
- freshly grated nutmeg
- 2 egg yolks, beaten
- 2 tbsp freshly grated Parmesan cheese
- salt and pepper

Scrub the potatoes and cook in boiling water until they are tender. While they are cooking, skin the sausages, break up the meat with a fork and fry until lightly browned. Drain the potatoes, peel, mash well and add the butter and parsley. Add the sausage meat, warmed milk, nutmeg and the remainder of the ingredients, beat well with a wooden spoon. Put the mixture into a buttered dish and bake in a fairly hot oven (190°C/375°F/Gas 5) for 30 minutes or until the top is brown.

POTATO OMELETTE
SERVES 2–3

- 2 tbsp butter
- 1–2 medium potatoes, peeled and diced
- few sprigs of rosemary, finely chopped
- 4 eggs
- 1½ tbsp cold water
- salt and pepper
- butter for frying

You can use raw or left-over potato for this. Melt butter in a pan and fry the potatoes, adding the rosemary just before the potato is cooked.

Break the eggs into a bowl and beat well with a fork. Add the water and seasoning. Put the butter into a pan, and when it begins to froth, add the omelette mixture. Leave just about 15 seconds before stirring it with the back of a fork, drawing up the cooked egg to allow the raw egg to cook. Do this a couple of times until the omelette is just cooked. Put the potato mixture in the middle, fold the omelette over and serve at once. Omelettes do not hold and are only good if they are eaten straight from the pan.

ROMAN GNOCCHI
SERVES 6 AS A STARTER,
4 AS A MAIN COURSE

This is another of Fergus's recipes which he cooked a lot when he lived in Italy. It is a simple one, and served with melting butter and good freshly grated Parmesan, it is delicious.

- 900 g/2 lb floury potatoes such as Queens
- salt and pepper
- 225 g/8 oz/2 cups flour
- 4 tbsp butter, melted
- 55 g/2 oz/½ cup freshly grated Parmesan cheese

Peel the potatoes and boil them until tender. Drain well and dry them thoroughly — it is important to get them as dry as possible. Mash them until smooth, put them in a mixing bowl and add salt and pepper. Then add the flour, little by little, to make a good firm dough.

Knead the dough for a couple of minutes and then divide it into 4 pieces. Roll out each piece into a cylinder shape about 1.2 cm/½ inch thick, cut into 2.5 cm/1 inch pieces and pinch them in the middle. Flour lightly.

Bring a big pot of lightly salted water to the boil, and drop in as many of the gnocchi as will comfortably fit. Boil them rapidly until they rise to the surface. Lift them out, drain them thoroughly and put in a warmed dish. Pour over the melted butter and cover generously with Parmesan cheese. Place them in a hot oven for a couple of minutes to allow the cheese to melt slightly, then serve.

POTATO PIZZA WITH MOZZARELLA
SERVES 4

This is really easy and quick to make and we all love it. You can, of course, add all sorts of extras like ham or anchovies. Sometimes I put anchovies on one quarter, ham on another and spinach on another, just to accommodate various tastes within the household. I use parsley and oregano together. If you cook in a stove such as a Stanley or an Aga, put the baking sheet on the floor of the top oven so that the bottom of the pizza base will be really crisp.

The base

- 675 g/1½ lb floury potatoes
- 4–5 tbsp oil
- salt and pepper

The topping

- 450 g/1 lb tomatoes
- chopped oregano or parsley
- salt and pepper
- 170 g/6 oz Mozzarella cheese
- 55 g/2 oz/½ cup freshly grated Parmesan cheese
- 12 black olives, pitted and quartered

To make the base

Wash the potatoes and boil them in their jackets until tender. Drain them well, cool, peel and mash them until they are quite smooth. Add enough oil to make a smooth mixture, then add the salt and pepper. Lightly brush a baking sheet with oil and sprinkle with flour. Spread the potato dough in a large even round on the baking sheet.

The topping

Peel the tomatoes, liquidise them with oregano or parsley and spread on top of the base. Season well. Slice the Mozzarella finely, cut each slice in half and lay it on top, followed by the Parmesan cheese and the olives. Drizzle a little olive oil on top and bake in a fairly hot oven (190°C/375°F/Gas 5) for about 15–20 minutes or until the cheese is melting and just beginning to brown.

4

Side Dishes

Sserve most of these dishes as an accompaniment to a meat, fish or vegetarian main course, but some make a great main course in themselves, served with good green vegetables or a fresh salad.

Colcannon

Colcannon is traditionally a Hallowe'en dish. In our house, as children, coins were sometimes wrapped in tin foil and mixed in — probably not very hygienic and wouldn't be allowed these days, but good fun. Colcannon is good any time of the year and best made with floury potatoes such as Home Guard in the earlies and Kerr's or Golden Wonders from the main crop.

COLCANNON 1
SERVES 4–6

There are all sorts of slight variations of colcannon but this is the one we always cooked. I like 'real' cabbage such as York, rather than the flavourless hard white heads common nowadays. Kale can be used instead of cabbage, and sometimes other root vegetables such as carrots or parsnips are added. My children eat colcannon on its own and can't get it often enough — partly because they hope to find a fortune wrapped in foil!

- 900 g/2 lb potatoes
- 1 small head of cabbage
- 300 ml/½ pint/1¼ cups milk (approximately)
- salt and pepper
- 6 tbsp butter

Scrub and boil the potatoes in a saucepan of salted water for about 30 minutes, or until just done. Wash the cabbage, remove the white core, discard, and chop the leaves well. Cook in a small amount of boiling water for about 4 minutes, or until just tender — do not let cabbage over-cook and become soggy. Drain the potatoes, peel and mash them. Bring the milk to almost boiling and add enough to the potatoes to make a soft but not runny con-sistency. Add the cabbage, mix well, season and serve in a warmed dish. Make a well in the centre, add the butter and serve immediately.

COLCANNON 2
SERVES 4–6

This is an old recipe for colcannon using parsley and onion in place of cabbage or kale.

- 6 medium potatoes
- 1 large bunch of parsley
- pinch of bread soda
- 2 tbsp butter
- 1 small onion, finely chopped
- 120 ml/4 fl oz/½ cup milk

Boil and mash the potatoes. Tie the parsley in a bunch, wash and put in a saucepan of boiling water to which a pinch of bread soda has been added. Boil for 3 minutes and drain. Remove the stalks, chop well and add to the mashed potatoes. Add the butter and onion to the milk, bring to the boil and simmer for 5 minutes. Add to the potatoes and mix well with a fork. Serve in a hot dish with a knob of butter in the centre.

Champ

Champ is a very old dish that is cooked all over the country. Once more, it has many variations depending on where you got the recipe from. It is traditionally made using onions, but in fact you can substitute a whole range of things for the onions — young nettles, parsley, leeks, herbs or chives. I often make it with leeks and streaky rashers fried in their own fat first, then broken into the champ: it is terrific. Again, floury potatoes are best.

CHAMP

SERVES 4–6

- 900 g/2 lb potatoes
- 110 g/4 oz big scallions (US green onions)
- 300 ml/½ pint/1¼ cups milk
- salt and pepper
- 110 g/4 oz/8 tbsp butter

Scrub and boil the potatoes for about 30 minutes until they are cooked. Chop the scallions and simmer in half the milk for about 5 minutes. Strain them, reserving the milk. Peel and mash the potatoes with the scallions, add the milk from the scallions and as much of the remaining milk as you need to make a soft, light mixture. Season, put into a warm dish, make a well in the centre, add the butter and serve.

Boxty

Boxty originates from the midlands of Ireland, and waxy or 'wet' potatoes can be used quite happily. It is a fine dish and many ingredients can be added to the traditional basic recipe to make it a meal in itself. Some boxty is boiled, some done on the pan; some recipes include flour, others do not. Many call for a mixture of mashed potatoes and raw grated potatoes; others add an egg to bind the mixture. Some recipes are very like what is known as rosti in other countries — but Irish boxty is special.

NANCY'S BOXTY
SERVES 4–6

My husband is from Leitrim, a boxty stronghold, and recalls his aunt, Nancy Geelan, cooking wonderful boxty. This is her recipe and it is very good.

- 8 big potatoes
- 110 g/4 oz/1 cup flour
- 1 level tsp bread soda
- 225 ml/8 fl oz/1 cup milk
- pinch of salt
- 2 tbsp butter

Scrub the potatoes and peel them if they are old. Grate into a large dish using the fine side of the grater. Drain the potato into a clean cloth to remove the excess liquid. Add the flour, bread soda, milk and salt and mix well with a wooden spoon. Melt the butter on a heavy frying pan. When it is bubbling, pour on the mixture. Cook, turning until brown on both sides. Serve at once with more butter.

BOXTY 2
SERVES 4–6

This is a quick and easy pan recipe for boxty.

- 900 g/2 lb potatoes
- 2 tsp white flour
- salt
- butter or bacon fat

Scrub and grate the potatoes into a clean cloth — you can peel them if you like but there is no need, unless the skin looks unpleasant. Let it sit for a while, then drain off any liquid before adding the flour and salt. Pat it into one big cake the size of your pan and leave it fairly thick, about 2–2.5 cm/¾–1 inch. Melt the butter until it begins to foam, then add the boxty. Let it cook for about 30 minutes, turning once. Turn it by removing the pan from the heat, putting a large plate upside-down on the pan and turning it over. Then slip the boxty back on the pan and let it cook until both sides are golden.

SLICED POTATOES WITH GARLIC
SERVES 6

These potatoes are quick to prepare and quick to cook; great when you are in a hurry. It is probably the potato dish we eat most often in our house, and is Clare's favourite. It takes 5 minutes to prepare, looks sophisticated and tastes good.

- 1.1 kg/2½ lb potatoes, unpeeled
- 4 cloves of garlic, chopped
- 1 tbsp olive oil
- salt and pepper
- 1 tbsp butter

Scrub the potatoes thoroughly. Peel and chop the garlic. Put the garlic in a small saucepan with the olive oil and butter and heat until the butter has melted and is good and hot. Don't allow it to sizzle or brown. Slice the potatoes thinly and place in a well buttered 25.5 cm/10 inch pie or flan dish. Layer the potatoes, seasoning between each layer. Only go to three layers: any deeper makes them a bit soggy. Then pour over evenly the garlic, butter and oil. Place in a medium hot oven (190°C/375°F/Gas 5) for about 45 minutes, until the top is golden. If you cook in a stove like a Stanley or an Aga, put the dish on the bottom of the top oven. This way the bottom layer of the potatoes is as golden and crisp as the top.

CHÂTEAU POTATOES
SERVES 4–6

This rich potato dish is easy to make and goes well with Sunday roasts, and other special occasions.

- 900 g/2 lb new potatoes
- 4 tbsp butter
- salt and pepper

Scrub the potatoes and dry them well on a tea towel. Melt the butter in a wide saucepan, add the potatoes and cook over a medium heat, turning frequently, until they are brown. Add salt and pepper, place in a roasting pan and cook in a fairly hot oven (200°C/400°F/Gas 6) for 10–12 minutes. Serve in a warm dish.

POTATOES WITH BUTTERMILK
SERVES 4

This delicious recipe was given to me by a friend, Elaine Hartigan. She quite rightly suggested serving it with bacon, a perfect combination.

- 8 medium potatoes
- 225 ml/8 fl oz/1 cup cream
- 225 ml/8 fl oz/1 cup buttermilk
- 2 tsp French mustard
- salt and pepper
- 110 g/4 oz white Cheddar cheese
- 30 g/1 oz freshly grated Parmesan cheese

Clean the potatoes and parboil for about 15 minutes.

Drain, peel and halve them, and place flat-side down in a buttered baking dish. Mix the cream, buttermilk and mustard in a bowl, season, and pour over the potatoes. Grate the Cheddar cheese on top, followed by the Parmesan. Bake in a fairly hot oven (190°C/375°F/Gas 5) for 30–40 minutes. The buttermilk and cheese blend into the potatoes and they become crusty on top.

POTATOES AND MUSHROOMS
SERVES 4

You can use button mushrooms in this but they can be flavourless; field mushrooms are better, if you can get them.

- 900 g/2 lb medium-sized potatoes
- 225 g/8 oz field mushrooms
- 2 tbsp butter
- 2 tbsp flour
- 300 ml/½ pint/1¼ cups milk and 300 ml/½ pint/1¼ cups potato water
- salt and pepper
- pinch of freshly grated nutmeg
- 2 tbsp cream or yoghurt

Peel and quarter the potatoes and trim the cut edges with a potato peeler. Cook gently in boiling water until just tender. Drain the water and reserve, allow the potatoes to dry. Wipe the mushrooms clean and leave the stalks on.

Toss the mushrooms in melted butter over a high heat. Mix in the flour, milk and potato water. Add seasoning, bring to

the boil and add the potatoes.
Cover the pot and cook for
about 10 minutes. Stir in
the nutmeg and cream
or yoghurt just before
serving.

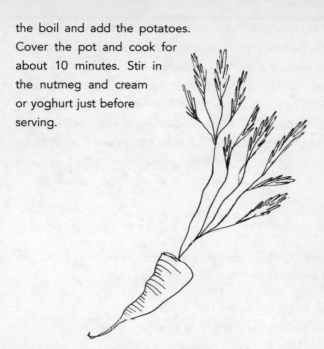

PURÉED POTATOES AND CARROTS
SERVES 4–6

We make this when we haven't quite enough potatoes or
quite enough carrots, but between the two we have plenty.

- 340 g/³⁄₄ lb carrots
- 570 g/1¼ lb potatoes
- 2 tbsp butter
- ¼ tsp grated nutmeg
- 110 ml/4 fl oz/½ cup hot milk

Trim the ends of the carrots and scrape them with a knife. Cut them into 2.5 cm/1 inch lengths. Peel and dice the potatoes. Put carrots and potatoes into cold salted water. Bring to the boil and simmer for 15–20 minutes until they are tender. Be careful not to overcook. Purée the vegetables or put through a coarse sieve. Return to a clean saucepan. Add the butter, nutmeg and seasoning and return to the heat. Beat in the hot milk with a wooden spoon. Serve immediately.

POTATO GRATIN
SERVES 6

Potato gratin made the following way can easily be served as a main course. It is rich and very good.

- 110 g/4 oz cream cheese
- 110 g/4 oz Parmesan or Gruyère cheese
- 150 ml/¼ pint/⅔ cups cream
- 3 eggs
- 50 ml/2 fl oz/¼ cup top-of-the-bottle milk
- a little rosemary or thyme
- salt and pepper
- 2 tsp freshly grated nutmeg
- 675 g/1½ lb potatoes

Beat the cream cheese, cheese and cream together, then beat in the eggs. Add the top-of-the-bottle milk and herbs, season with salt, pepper and nutmeg. Peel and grate the potatoes. You can leave the potatoes unpeeled, but the peel looks a bit off-putting in the finished dish. Sprinkle with salt and pepper and leave to stand for 5–10 minutes. Drain off the liquid and put the potatoes into a buttered gratin dish. Pour over the cheese and cream and cook in a fairly hot oven (200°C/400°F/Gas 6) for 40–45 minutes.

SCALLOPED POTATOES

SERVES 4

You can use ham or bacon in this recipe but bacon gives it a better flavour and turns it into a meal in itself.

- 675 g/1½ lb potatoes
- salt and pepper
- 75 g/3 oz strong Cheddar cheese
- 75 g/3 oz chopped cooked bacon or ham
- fresh herbs such as a little sage, thyme and parsley
- 450 ml/16 fl oz/2 cups milk
- 4 tbsp butter

Scrub the potatoes and slice them thinly. Layer them in a greased oven dish. Add salt, pepper, cheese, bacon and herbs followed by another layer of potatoes. Repeat each layer, finishing with a layer of potatoes. Add the milk, dot with butter and cook in a medium oven (180°C/350°F/ Gas 4) until the potatoes are cooked and the top is crisp — about 45 minutes.

POTATOES LAYERED WITH CHEESE
SERVES 6

- 900 g/2 lb potatoes
- 2 eggs
- 120 ml/4 fl oz/½ cup milk
- 120 ml/4 fl oz/½ cup cream
- 3 big cloves of garlic, crushed
- salt and pepper
- 170 g/6 oz good Cheddar cheese, grated
- ½ tsp grated nutmeg
- 4 scallions (US green onions), finely chopped

Scrub the potatoes well and slice thinly. Beat the eggs with the milk, cream, garlic, salt and pepper, half the cheese and the grated nutmeg. Add the potatoes and scallions, and then put the mixture into a well buttered dish. Sprinkle the remaining cheese on top. Cook for about 40 minutes in a medium hot oven (180°C/350°F/Gas 4), taking care that the cheese on top does not burn.

BAKED POTATO SHAPES
SERVES 4

These are irresistible and children love them. Using a scone or biscuit cutter, they can be made into shapes like fish to serve with fish, or trains etc.

- 675 g/1½ lb old potatoes
- 2 tbsp butter
- 1 medium onion, finely chopped
- 2 tbsp chopped chives
- 30 g/1 oz Cheddar cheese
- salt and pepper

Scrub the potatoes and parboil them until almost done — about 15 minutes. Allow them to cool, then peel and grate them with a coarse grater. Melt the butter and cook the onion until they are soft but not brown. Mix with the grated potatoes, grated cheese, chives and seasoning. Spoon into about 8 shapes or mounds. Cook for about 15 minutes in a hot oven (220°C/425°F/Gas 7) until they are golden and crispy on the outside.

FRIED NEW POTATOES
WITH CHEESE
SERVES 4

This is a great recipe, in content not unlike the roast potatoes with Parmesan, but done in the pan they have quite a different flavour.

- 675 g/1½ lb small new potatoes
- 2 tbsp olive oil
- 55 g/2 oz/½ cup Parmesan cheese
- salt and pepper

Scrub and cook the potatoes in boiling salted water until tender, about 10 minutes. Heat the oil in a large heavy frying pan, add the potatoes and toss in the oil for about 5 minutes. Stir in the finely grated cheese; cook for a further 1–2 minutes until the cheese begins to blend but doesn't get tough. Season with very little salt and pepper.

ROSTI POTATOES
SERVES 4

- 675 g/1½ lb waxy potatoes
- 2 tbsp cooking oil
- 4 tbsp butter
- salt and pepper

Scrub the potatoes and parboil them until they are almost done — about 15 minutes. Allow to cool, peel and grate with a coarse grater. Meantime, in a heavy-based or iron pan, heat the oil. Allow it to stand for a while, pour it off and wipe the pan with a paper towel. Heat 2 tbsp of the butter and add the potatoes in a 2.5 cm/1 inch layer. Sprinkle with salt and pepper. Press them down into the pan with a flat spatula. Allow to cook for 10 minutes.

When they are golden brown, cover the pan with a plate as large as or larger than the pan, quickly turn it upside-down on to the plate. Replace the pan on the heat and slip the 'pancake' back on to it. Add a further 2 tbsp of butter around the edge of the pan, letting it melt into the potato. Add more butter if you need to. Continue to cook, pressing it down occasionally until it is ready. Serve on a hot plate and slice like a cake.

POTATOES IN CREAM SAUCE
SERVES 4

This recipe is very rich, one to cook for a special occasion. It goes well with fairly plain dishes.

- 4 large potatoes
- 225 ml/8 fl oz/1 cup heavy cream
- 1/3 tsp freshly grated nutmeg
- salt
- pinch of cayenne pepper
- 110 g/4 oz/1 cup chopped scallions (US green onions)

Peel the potatoes and rinse. Slice into quarters lengthways and cut into 2.5 cm/1 inch lengths. Put the potatoes in a saucepan of salted water and bring to the boil. Simmer for about 5 minutes and drain. Add the cream, nutmeg, salt, cayenne and scallions. Bring to the boil, cover and cook for about 4 minutes until almost done. Season and boil uncovered to allow the cream to thicken, about 1 minute.

POTATOES BAKED IN SMITHWICKS
SERVES 4

Potatoes with beer is not a combination which normally springs to mind, but this recipe is very good and you can use any kind of potato.

- 900 g/2 lb potatoes
- 2 large onions, thinly sliced
- salt and pepper
- 225 ml/8 fl oz/1 cup Smithwicks or ale/lager
- 4 tbsp butter, very cold
- 150 ml/¼ pint/⅔ cup cream

Scrub the potatoes well and slice them thinly. Place alternate slices of onion and potato in a buttered dish, packed closely together. Salt each layer lightly. Add the beer and shavings of butter evenly distributed. Bake in a hot oven (220°C/425°F/Gas 7) for 10 minutes; reduce the temperature to a moderate oven (180°C/350°F/Gas 4) for a further 40 minutes. About 10 minutes before the end, pour the cream evenly over the top, then return to the oven.

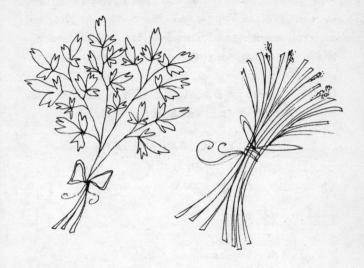

POTATO AND CELERIAC GALETTE
SERVES 4–6

This recipe comes from a magazine which is so dog-eared it is unidentifiable.

- 900 g/2 lb old potatoes
- 900 g/2 lb celeriac
- 2 cloves of garlic
- freshly ground nutmeg
- salt and pepper
- 75 g/3 oz/6 tbsp butter, melted
- parsley or chopped chives to garnish

Grease and line the base of two 20 cm/8 inch round tins. Peel and slice the potatoes and celeriac very thinly. Layer them in the bottom of the tins with the crushed garlic, nutmeg and seasoning and press down firmly as you layer. The tins should be full. Pour half the butter on each one. Cover with foil and cook in a very hot oven (200°C/ 400°F/Gas 6) for about 1 hour, or until cooked. Turn on to a hot plate, garnish with parsley or chopped chives and serve.

POTATO PARMESAN
SERVES 4

This is a strong, rich potato dish and is excellent with game.

- 4 large potatoes
- 2 tbsp butter
- 30 g/1 oz Parmesan cheese, grated
- 2 egg yolks
- large pinch of nutmeg
- salt and pepper
- 2 egg whites
- breadcrumbs
- oil for frying

Peel and wash the potatoes, quarter and boil until soft. Drain and mash. Add the butter, cheese, egg yolks, nutmeg, salt and pepper and mix well. When cool, shape into 5 cm/2 inch rounds. Coat with lightly beaten egg white and crumbs. Heat the oil and cook for about 5 minutes, turning once, until golden. Remove from the pan and drain on warmed kitchen paper.

BAKER'S POTATOES
SERVES 4–6

This recipe is very good with roast pork together with a stuffing using the same herbs.

- 4 medium potatoes
- 2 tbsp olive oil
- 1 large onion, finely chopped
- clove of garlic
- 400 ml/14 fl oz/1¾ cups chicken stock
- ½ tsp sage and thyme mixed

Heat the oil in a shallow, heavy-based pan, stir in the onion and soften over a slow heat. Wash and dry the potatoes, slice very thinly. Mash the garlic clove with a little salt, add it and the potato slices to the onion, coating the slices with the oil. Barely cover with the stock. Scatter the herbs on top, cover with foil and place in a fairly hot oven (200°C/400°F/Gas 6) for approximately 40 minutes.

POTATOES WITH GARLIC AND BAY LEAVES
SERVES 4–6

The bay leaves in this recipe give a lovely flavour which seems to seep through in the cooking.

- 5 cloves of garlic
- 425 ml/¾ pint/1¾ cups water
- 900 g/2 lb potatoes
- 4–5 tbsp olive oil
- 4 bay leaves

Cook the garlic cloves in the water, simmering for about 15 minutes. Lift out the garlic, push the soft flesh from the skin, and purée through a sieve back into the water. While the garlic is cooking, scrub the potatoes, slice thinly and dry. Coat an oven dish with the olive oil, pack in half the potatoes, add the bay leaves and then the remaining potatoes. Pour over the garlic water to cover them, and drizzle the remaining olive oil on top. Cook in a fairly hot oven (200°C/400°F/Gas 6) for 45–50 minutes until done.

POTATO, GRUYÈRE AND CELERY
SERVES 4

- 675 g/1½ lb potatoes
- 150 ml/¼ pint/⅔ cup cream
- 110 g/4 oz/8 tbsp butter
- 3 tbsp chopped onion
- 3 sticks celery, chopped
- 4–6 tbsp freshly grated Gruyère cheese
- salt
- pinch of cayenne
- freshly grated nutmeg

Peel and cook the potatoes in boiling, salted water for about 15–20 minutes until just tender. Drain and mash with the cream. Meantime, melt half the butter in a heavy pan and cook the onion and celery until they are transparent; add to the potatoes. Mix in the cheese and season with salt, cayenne and freshly grated nutmeg to taste. Melt the remaining butter in a frying pan, add the potato and celery mixture and spread into a flat cake. Cook for about 15 minutes, turn it on to a plate, slip it back on to the pan, add the rest of the butter and cook for a further 10 minutes until it is golden. Cut straight away and serve.

GARLIC POTATOES WITH CREAM
SERVES 6

My friend Denise Barnes gave me this recipe and it is unlikely you could find anything with so many calories per gram or so indulgently delicious.

- 1.1 kg/2½ lb potatoes
- 2 large cloves of garlic
- 4 tbsp butter
- salt and pepper
- 600–900 ml/1–1½ pints/2½–3¾ cups cream

Peel the potatoes and slice thinly. Finely chop the garlic and mix with the butter. Using a deep well-buttered oven dish, layer the potatoes, salt, pepper and garlic butter, until all the potatoes are used up. Pour over enough cream to cover the potatoes, and cook in a medium oven (180°C/350°F/Gas 4) for 1–1¼ hours until the potatoes are tender and the top is golden brown.

SPINACH AND YOGHURT POTATO SKINS
SERVES 4

This is a recipe given to me by my Australian friend, Monica McInerney, an enthusiastic cook. We always include a new recipe or two in our letters to one another. This one arrived last year and has become a favourite.

- 4 large potatoes
- 3 tbsp oil
- 1 clove of garlic, crushed
- 450 g/1 lb packet frozen spinach
- 2 tbsp plain yoghurt
- 55 g/2 oz/1 cup dry breadcrumbs, brown or white
- 2 tbsp butter, melted

Use good floury potatoes such as Queens, scrub them well and place in a hot oven (220°C/425°F/Gas 7) to bake for about 1 hour. Cut into quarters and spoon out the centre into a bowl, leaving a little on the skins. Brush the skins with oil and put them back on the oven tray to cook for a further 10 minutes.

Heat 2 tbsp of oil in a pan, add the garlic and drained spinach, and cook for about 3 minutes, stirring it. Take the pan off the heat, add the flesh from the potatoes, the yoghurt and half the breadcrumbs, and allow the mixture to cool a little. Add the remaining breadcrumbs to the melted butter and keep aside. Spoon the spinach mixture into the potato skins, put on the baking sheet and sprinkle with the breadcrumbs and butter mixture. Put them back in the oven and cook for about 10 minutes or until lightly browned.

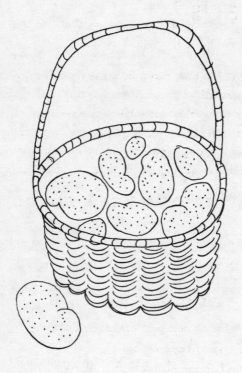

5
Salads

One of the best things about summer is the enormous choice of fresh, crisp salad leaves. The texture and flavour of different leaves and freshly picked herbs in season is spectacular. Potatoes give real body to a salad making it almost a meal in itself. The recipes below combine potatoes with all sorts of summer salads, and they're all delicious.

POTATO AND CHIVE SALAD
SERVES 4

The dressing on this salad is a pleasant change from the traditional oil, vinegar, garlic, salt and pepper. A mix of summer salad leaves is best but any available green leaves will do, the fresher the better.

- 675 g/1½ lb new potatoes, scrubbed lightly
- 6 tbsp good vegetable oil
- 2 tbsp extra virgin olive oil
- 2 tbsp red wine vinegar
- 1 tbsp Irish mustard
- sea-salt and freshly ground black pepper
- 1 tbsp chopped chives
- mixed salad leaves

Cover the potatoes with boiling water and add the mint. Return to the boil and when cooked, drain and cut into bite-sized pieces. Leave aside to cool.

Whisk the oils, vinegar and mustard, add salt and pepper. Pour the dressing over the potatoes, add the chives, toss with the salad leaves and serve.

POTATO SALAD WITH ROSEMARY AND CHEESE
SERVES 4

This salad is filling and makes a meal in itself, accompanied by a good green salad of fresh leaves.

- 900 g/2 lb new or peeled old potatoes
- 6 tbsp extra virgin olive oil
- 1 medium-sized onion, chopped
- generous sprig of rosemary
- 1 egg yolk
- 2 tbsp vinegar
- salt and pepper
- 2 tomatoes
- 1 dozen black olives
- 75 g/3 oz mature Cheddar, grated

Cook the new potatoes in boiling water and drain when ready. Heat the olive oil in a pan, add the chopped onion and half the rosemary leaves, and cook the onion until lightly browned. Drain the oil and put it to one side to cool.

Beat the egg till frothy, then pour in the oil slowly, taking care not to curdle it; add salt and pepper and vinegar to taste. Chop the tomatoes and the potatoes, place in a large salad bowl. Add the onions, olives and cheese, pour the dressing over and sprinkle with the rest of the rosemary. Serve while still warm.

NEW POTATOES WITH FRENCH DRESSING, MINT AND CHIVES
SERVES 4

The herbs in this recipe blend well with the French dressing although you can, of course, substitute your own favourite herbs. Choose small same-size potatoes.

- 675 g/1½ lb new potatoes
- fistful of mint leaves
- 1 tbsp chives
- 2 tbsp extra virgin olive oil
- 2 tbsp sunflower oil
- 1 tbsp red wine vinegar
- 1 clove of garlic, crushed
- salt and pepper

Scrub and steam the potatoes for about 10 minutes until tender, making sure the pot doesn't boil dry. Tear the mint into strips, and chop the chives finely. Then make the French dressing: mix the oils, vinegar, garlic, salt and pepper. When the potatoes are cooked toss them in the dressing, add the mint and chives and serve.

WARM POTATO SALAD WITH PARMA HAM AND PARSLEY

SERVES 4

The Parma ham gives this salad a lovely flavour. I always wait a few minutes to let the potatoes soak up the dressing before serving.

- 675 g/1½ lb new or peeled old potatoes
- 3 slices Parma ham
- 2 tbsp extra virgin olive oil
- 2 tbsp red wine vinegar
- 1 tbsp chives or spring onions
- salt and pepper
- 3–4 sprigs of parsley, chopped

Boil the potatoes in salted water. Meantime, mix the oil and vinegar together. Chop the Parma ham into small strips and put it in a large serving dish. Add the oil and vinegar, chives or spring onions, salt and pepper. When the potatoes are cooked, put them in the salad bowl with the parsley. Toss carefully so they are all covered in the dressing. Leave for at least 5 minutes to let the potatoes absorb the dressing, then serve.

POTATO AND PARSLEY SALAD
SERVES 6

- 675 g/1½ lb small new potatoes or floury old potatoes
- 4 good fistfuls of flat-leafed parsley
- 55 g/2 oz Parmesan cheese in the block

For the dressing

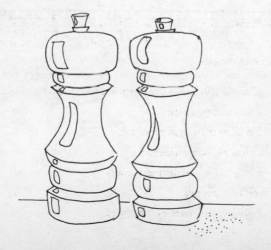

- small clove of garlic, mashed almost to liquid with the edge of a knife
- 2 tsp good white wine
- 3 tbsp good olive oil
- 1 tbsp sunflower oil
- salt and pepper

Scrub the potatoes well. If you are using new potatoes, steam them until they are just cooked. If you are using old potatoes, boil them carefully in salted water with the cover off. Chop the parsley coarsely. Make the French dressing by mixing the remaining ingredients in a large salad bowl. When the potatoes are cooked, allow them to cool a little and then toss them in the dressing with parsley, making sure they are well coated. With a potato peeler, shave the Parmesan on top of the salad and serve.

WARM POTATO SALAD WITH CRISPY RASHERS AND ROCKET
SERVES 4

The vinegar is important in this recipe to bring out the flavour of the ingredients.

- 12 medium-sized scrubbed new potatoes
- 6 slices of streaky bacon
- 2 tbsp extra virgin olive oil
- 2 tbsp good wine vinegar

- 1 large handful of rocket
- 4 tbsp chopped chives or green onion tops

While the potatoes are cooking in boiling water, chop the bacon and cook in a large frying pan until crisp. Drain on kitchen paper. Mix the oil, vinegar, rocket, scallions or chives and bacon in a large serving dish. Add the potatoes, stir and serve.

NEW POTATOES IN PARSLEY BUTTER
SERVES 4

Another simple but terrific potato recipe. The parsley butter gives the potatoes a melt-in-the-mouth flavour.

- 900 g/2 lb scrubbed new potatoes
- 4–6 tbsp butter
- large sprig of parsley, chopped
- salt and pepper

Put the potatoes in a large saucepan of salted boiling water for about 15 minutes until cooked, then drain. Melt the butter in a small saucepan, add the parsley, salt and pepper, and stir well to make the parsley butter. Place the cooked potatoes in a warmed serving dish, pour the parsley butter over and serve.

MINTED POTATO SALAD
SERVES 4

This lovely salad can be made a little in advance and kept in the fridge. You could use a little less lemon if you find it a bit sharp.

- 450 g/1 lb small potatoes, halved
- 6 tbsp lemon juice — or less if you find the lemon too sharp
- 4 tbsp olive oil
- salt and pepper
- 1 small cucumber, chopped
- 1 stick celery, chopped
- 4 big scallions (US green onions)
- 110 g/4 oz/2 cups parsley, chopped
- 3 tbsp fresh mint, chopped

Boil the potatoes until just tender, drain, dry and cut in half. In a large bowl make the dressing using the lemon, olive oil and salt and pepper. Add all the other ingredients and mix well, making sure that the mint and parsley are well distributed. Taste for seasoning.

DELICIOUS CHEESE AND POTATO SALAD

SERVES 4

This recipe is made with Gorgonzola or any creamy, strong cheese. I sometimes use Cashel Blue which is very good.

- 450 g/1 lb new potatoes
- 30 g/1 oz hazel nuts, toasted and chopped coarsely
- 2 tbsp hazelnut oil
- 2 tbsp good olive oil
- 200 g/7 oz Gorgonzola or similar cheese
- salt and pepper

Scrub the potatoes well and cook in boiling salted water until tender. While they are cooking, toast the hazelnuts by putting them in a medium oven for a few minutes; rub them in a clean tea towel to remove the skins, chop and mix with the oil. When the potatoes are cooked, drain and cut in half. Roughly chop the cheese and add it, with the potatoes, to the hazelnuts, and mix well. Season carefully and serve immediately.

POTATO SALAD WITH ANCHOVIES
SERVES 4

If you like anchovies you will love this dish. As always with anchovies, watch the seasoning — they are very salty and the chances are that you will not need to add salt when it comes to seasoning.

- 675 g/1½ lb firm potatoes such as King Edwards or Roosters
- seasoning

For the dressing
- 1 tbsp anchovy paste
- 4–6 anchovy fillets
- ½ small onion, finely chopped
- 1–2 cloves of garlic
- 1 tbsp capers
- 150 ml/¼ pint/⅔ cup white wine

Wash the potatoes and boil in salted water until cooked.
While they are cooking, put the anchovy paste into a bowl,
add the anchovies with their oil, and mix well with a wooden
spoon or salad server. Add the onion, capers, garlic and
wine. When the potatoes are cooked, peel and cut into
cubes. Add to the dressing while they are still warm. Cover
and stand for at least 15 minutes before serving.

6
Potato Cakes

Potato cakes are a great traditional Irish dish and a great favourite in most households. They are good for breakfast, lunch or anytime. It seems there are about 350 different recipes for them, each one *the* correct one, some quite rich and some very simple. It is a great way of using left-over potatoes, or you can simply add a few extra to the dinner pot in order to have them ready for the next day. You will find the more you cook them the more you will adjust your recipe to what is in the fridge.

SIMPLE POTATO CAKES
SERVES 4

- 225 g/8 oz/1 cup mashed potatoes
- 110 g/4 oz/1 cup flour
- 110 g/4 oz/8 tbsp butter
- salt and pepper
- a little butter for cooking

Use good floury potatoes such as Kerr's Pinks, or Golden Wonders in winter. Mash the potatoes, add the flour, softened butter and seasoning. Knead together until it has a rough dough-like consistency. Roll out and slice or cut into 10 cm/4 inch rounds. Heat the butter in a pan and fry them until they are golden brown, turning once. You may need a little more butter when you turn them. If you do, turn the potato cakes, and allow the butter to seep down underneath them. Serve immediately with a knob of melting butter.

PARMESAN POTATO CAKES
SERVES 4

Parmesan is not a traditional addition to potato cakes but it works really well. We often have these for lunch served with a simple parsley or green salad.

- 225 g/8 oz/1 cup mashed potatoes
- 110 g/4 oz/1 cup flour
- 75 g/3 oz/6 tbsp butter
- 45 g/1½ oz good Parmesan cheese, freshly grated
- salt and pepper
- a little butter for cooking

Boil the potatoes, peel and mash. Add the flour, butter, Parmesan and seasoning. Knead to a rough dough-like consistency and roll. Cut into shapes and fry in a pan until golden, turning once. Again, if you need more butter, add it to the side of the pan and allow it to seep under the cakes. Serve immediately.

THEODORA FITZGIBBON'S
POTATO CAKE

This recipe comes from Theodora FitzGibbon's *Irish Traditional Food*; she says it is a very old country method. Theodora's recipe uses chopped peel, but my children won't eat it with peel so I either substitute another dried fruit or omit it. I prefer it plain with butter.

She also suggests using finely chopped onions which are very tasty. Fry them gently in a little butter to soften.

- 225 g/8 oz cooked mashed potatoes
- about 3 tbsp flour
- 1 large egg, separated
- 2 tbsp melted butter
- 2 tbsp chopped peel — optional
- pinch of salt

Mash the potatoes in a bowl and add sufficient flour to form a firm dough. Beat the egg yolk and egg white separately. Blend in a little over half the butter, add the beaten egg yolk and finally add the stiffly beaten egg white. Season well and shape into a round cake the size of your pan. Butter a heavy pan (a solid non-stick pan is good for all these recipes, just make sure it has a good base) and add the mixture.

Cover and cook for about 30 minutes over a moderate heat. Serve it hot.

SWEET POTATO CAKES OR LATKES
SERVES 4

This is a recipe that a neighbour gave me when I lived in America, and all my family love it. I think it is a Jewish recipe.

- 900 g/2 lb potatoes
- 55 g/2 oz/½ cup self-raising flour
- salt and pepper
- 1 beaten egg
- light oil for frying
- 3 tbsp caster sugar
- 1 tsp cinnamon

Peel the potatoes and grate into cold water. Strain and squeeze to get the water out. Place in a bowl, add the flour, seasoning and beaten egg and mix well. Heat the oil in a good pan and carefully drop a tablespoon of the mixture on to the oil; fry until golden, turning once. Drain them well on warmed kitchen paper or newspaper. Dust them with the mixed sugar and cinnamon and serve hot.

POTATO AND APPLE CAKE

This recipe is one of Theodora FitzGibbon's which I cut out of the *Irish Times*.

- 450 g/1 lb freshly-made mashed potato
- 1 heaped tbsp butter
- 2 tsp white sugar
- pinch of ginger
- 3 tbsp flour
- 900 g/2 lb cooking apples, peeled and sliced
- 1 tbsp brown sugar

Blend the hot potato with the butter, white sugar and ginger. Add enough flour to make a workable dough, and knead until smooth. Roll out into two rounds, one a little bigger than the other. Put the larger round on a piece of greaseproof paper, cover with the sliced apple and sprinkle with brown sugar. Dampen the edges of the dough and put the smaller round on top, press down to seal the edges. Prick all over with a fork and make a small cut in the middle. Cook in a medium oven (180°C/350°F/Gas 4) for about 35 minutes until a nice golden brown. Serve hot with brown sugar.

POTATO PANCAKES

SERVES 4–6

These are much nicer than they sound and are easy to make.
Serve them for lunch with apple sauce and a green salad.

- 900 g/2 lb potatoes, peeled and diced
- 120 ml/4 fl oz/½ cup milk
- ½ onion, finely chopped or grated
- 55 g/2 oz/½ cup flour
- 2 tsp salt
- 2 egg whites
- oil

Grate the potatoes with a fine grater on to a clean tea
towel and leave for about 10 minutes so that the liquid can

run off. Place in a bowl, stir in the milk and add the onion, flour and salt. Mix this very well, add the egg whites and mix again. Let this batter stand for 10 minutes. Heat the oil in a pan — be generous with the oil, you need lots to cook this properly. Spoon in about 2 tablespoons of the batter to make a small thickish pancake. You can cook as many of these together as your pan allows. After 2–3 minutes, turn them and fry for another 3 minutes. Put on a hot dish with warm kitchen paper or newspaper to drain.

SAVOURY POTATO STRAWS

These make a great snack, but you need to make plenty of them. Róisín de Buitlear gave me this recipe which came from the *Colour Book of Indian Cooking*.

- 2 medium potatoes
- oil for frying
- ½ tsp salt
- ¾ tsp caraway seeds
- pinch of cayenne

Peel and grate the potatoes on to a wooden board to allow them to dry. Heat the oil until it spits when you drop in a piece of potato, then add the potato and fry until golden brown. Drain well on warmed kitchen paper or newspaper. Combine the salt, caraway seeds and cayenne, sprinkle over the potatoes. These can be eaten hot or cold.

POTATO STICKS

These are quicker to make than they sound and are popular served on their own as something to nibble.

- ■ 170 g/6 oz floury potatoes
- ■ 170 g/6 oz/¾ cup butter
- ■ 170 g/6 oz/1½ cups plain flour
- ■ salt and pepper
- ■ 1 egg yolk
- ■ 2 tbsp top-of-the-bottle milk
- ■ poppy seeds/coarse sea-salt/caraway seeds

Peel the potatoes and boil in salted water until almost tender. Drain and allow to cool. Grate the potatoes coarsely, mix with the butter and flour and season well. Knead to a smooth dough and divide into four sections. Make a long roll with each section and cut into 16 finger-length pieces; score them across the top with a knife. Beat the egg yolk with the cream and brush the fingers with the mixture. Place on a floured baking sheet, sprinkle one-third of the fingers with caraway seeds, one-third with poppy seeds and the remainder with coarse sea-salt. Bake in a hot oven (200°C/400°F/Gas 6) for 10–12 minutes.

POTATO CROÛTONS

You never think to make croûtons with potatoes but just try
these with tomato or spinach soup — gorgeous!

- 2 potatoes
- oil for frying

Peel and parboil the potatoes. Drain and dice into small
cubes while they are still hot. Heat the oil well (don't be
mean with the quantity of oil you use) and fry until golden.

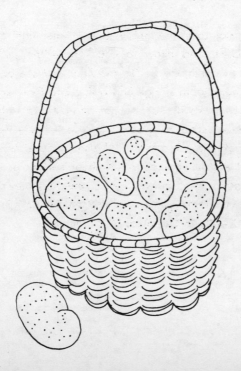

Index